Books by Wayne F. Hill and Cynthia J. Öttchen

Shakespeare's Insults

for

TEACHERS

SHAKESPEARE'S INSULTS FOR
TEACHERS

WAYNE F. HILL

AND

CYNTHIA J. ÖTTCHEN

—

ILLUSTRATIONS
BY
TOM LULEVITCH

CLARKSON POTTER/PUBLISHERS
NEW YORK

Published by Clarkson N. Potter/Publishers,
201 East 50th Street, New York, New York 10022.
Member of the Crown Publishing Group.

Random House, Inc.
New York, Toronto, London, Sydney, Auckland

http://www.randomhouse.com/

CLARKSON N. POTTER, POTTER, and colophon
are trademarks of Clarkson N. Potter, Inc.

Printed in the United States of America

Design by Alexander Knowlton
@ BEST Design Incorporated

Library of Congress Cataloging-in-Publication Data is
available upon request.

ISBN 0-517-70448-X

10   9   8   7   6   5   4   3   2   1

First Edition

This book is dedicated to an uncle,
two aunts, a mother, two sisters,
a sister-in-law, thirteen friends, and
our own two selves, all of whom have
taken a hand in teaching, and also
to an indistinct number of other
people we know personally as
having caught a whiff of education.
All but two of these have wished
to claim anonymity, and those two
are entertaining second thoughts
and dallying with pseudonyms.

Th'art a scholar; let us

therefore eat and drink.

TWELFTH NIGHT
2.3.13

CONTENTS

INTRODUCTION

> Ignorance is essential
> in the teaching profession.
> Without it teachers would
> not exist. But most teachers
> have forgotten the adage
> that ignorance is bliss
> and instead pin their
> hopes for civilization and
> the future squarely on
> education.

Actually, ignorance is the truly common experience of all humankind in every culture throughout history. Freedom from knowledge is unifying; it is contemporary humanity's one living link with the ancients and only sure connection with the future.

Computers can be knowledgeable; it takes a human mind to be ignorant.

Ignorance is as good as being fluent in every language and adept in every subject, for it crosses all speech barriers, transcends geographical remoteness, obviates unequal expertise, and is at home in the corridors of power. The community of not knowing encompasses old and young, great and small, rich and poor. Ignorance is a birthright, a political right, indeed, a social obligation. If endangered species, fossils, and crumbling architecture are protected by law, guarded in grim museums, and preserved to engender knowledge that normal people need never fear knowing, then obviously something as central as ignorance is a great lolling natural treasure. The pure expansive simplicity of dirt-dull, unspoiled ignorance is a thing of wonder.

In this delicate ecology, teachers are the civil engineers of the mental landscape. The mad road-makers are keen to move mountains, divert rivers, and chop down forests to tie up primal dumbness in concrete ribbons of education. Clearly this teacherly urge arouses controversy. Can the People-Who-

Know be trusted to represent the interests of the intellectually pure? Once lost, ignorance —like virginity—can never be recovered.

Ever eager to justify their expert role in society, educators admit the facts but have two ways of painting a happy face on the vacant noddle. The first is the easy argument that some ignorance is okay because even experts have more to learn, but this is timid at best. It weakly attempts to achieve the same end that is much better attained by sheer know-it-all arrogance. And the second argument, that at some point a person knows enough, is also sad, hopeful nonsense. This is only an excuse for quitting, giving out diplomas and degrees, and organizing amateur processionals in an attempt to dignify hyperbole.

Year after year, tremendous national resources are devoted to supporting these two arguments, neither of which is necessary. Ignorance itself would not pose an official problem at all if administrators of education did not define what levels of knowledge were required for us to qualify to be a certain age. Without them we might all grow happily old and dumb. Most of us will anyhow.

Teaching is therefore a struggle against nature, and students have a reponsibility to stand up and answer back. If native intellectual purity must be encroached upon, both sides had better have a voice in how it's done. Worthwhile learning requires conflict. Lecture halls and classrooms must echo with controversy between teacher and student. Students, with their taste for rebelliousness, have had the right idea, if not the professional sophisication, all along. If there is respect for anyone, let it be respect among worthy opponents.

For dramatic conflict William Shakespeare has no equal. Many a harassed student and harried teacher has wondered why we learn or teach Shakespeare after four hundred years. But until our own ground-breaking investigation, no one had bothered to wonder why his 38 plays contain nearly 10,000 insults, perfect for use in something other than a pop quiz. The compass point of education has shifted to a new direction. No longer is familiarity with Shakespeare an *end* to learning—that is to say, boring. The Bard is now a *means* of learning. Putting his insults to inventive use nurtures what all good students have always had—their instinctive combativeness and wicked imagination. In a completely new way, Shakespeare can prevent bad education. This approach is proven by successful classroom use of our previous books, *Shakespeare's Insults, Educating Your Wit,* and the accompanying teacher's guide *The Power of Language.*

Everyone in the world of education—whether teaching, having teaching performed on one's person, administering in some untidy corner of the education industry, or contributing bizarre parental behavior—is thrown into encounters that are natural opportunities for Shakespeare's insults.

TEACHERS AND ADMINISTRATORS

I wonder that you will

still be talking:

nobody marks you.

MUCH ADO ABOUT NOTHING
1. 1. 107–8

TEACHERS ARE REQUIRED to "get through the material." They are ruled by syllabus and curriculum. This is a major disadvantage, for the whole point of modern education is that there is an enormous difference between what teachers and students each bring to the classroom. Teachers want their pupils to learn, students are generally allergic to the whole process, and it's up to teachers to prevail. This compels them to adopt certain traits that, from their class's point of view, add up to being boring, tyrannical, and weird, and obviously leave them open to constructive criticism if not ridicule.

Students are not normal people, but like normal people, they invent insults every day for particular people or occasions. Rather than have Shakespeare forced down their throats, students have always gagged and resisted. Yawning while sitting in a classroom thee-ing and thou-ing their way aloud through a play, they have always picked out the most cutting bits, so that only the rude parts ever get beyond the classroom door. In a happy coincidence, many of them describe certain teachers perfectly.

When teachers can no longer teach, they

either teach teachers or administer. The immediate appeal of a career in administration is the absence of students, who are now reduced to statistics that can be safely moved around on flip charts and annual reports designed primarily for politicians who know even less about the real world than the administrator does.

But the principal attraction of slipping into administration is power. And that always takes the form of defending one's base of influence by obstructing good ideas and worthy projects.

BORING TEACHERS

THE ART OF BEING BORING is a sophisticated teaching technique borrowed from politics and religion. Successful techniques include speaking slowly and indistinctly. Irrelevance is absolutely vital and, with the help of the subject matter chosen for the purpose by curriculum committees, is relatively easy to achieve.

Cornford's *Microcosmographia Academica* advises "while you are engaged in Boring, it does not matter much what you talk about;

but, if possible, you should discourse upon the proper way of doing something you are notorious for doing badly yourself." Thus the old maxim "If you can't do, teach" suggests the wide range of possibilities many teachers have at their disposal for achieving high standards of boredom. They can drone on for hours about subjects they have never quite done or seen. The ironic corollary to these principles is that the teacher's agenda of forcing education on the pupil always assumes that the teacher knows best. This leaves everyone else in the classroom in the awkward position of not quite knowing what's going on. From there it is a short step to not caring what is going on.

Teachers who are not boring are likely to be in trouble with the administration for being too creative, too clever, and too well liked by their classes. They pose a threat to their duller colleagues; they find themselves in danger of losing their jobs. But it is danger and risk that get hearts pumping and blood flowing, and institutions of learning are anxious to avoid all this excitement. The vitalizing use of Shakespeare injects wit into boredom and generates interest, which is forbidden. The results could fire off in any direction like real life and, heaven spare us, might provoke enjoyment.

More of your conversation would infect my brain.

CORIOLANUS
2. 1. 93–94

(Your) reasons are as two grains of wheat hid in two bushels of chaff: you shall seek all day ere you find them, and when you have them, they are not worth the search.

THE MERCHANT OF VENICE
1. 1. 115–18

Will you credit this base drudge's words, That speaks he knows not what?

HENRY VI, PART 2
4. 2. 144–45

It will be prov'd to thy face that thou hast men about thee that usually talk of a noun, and a verb, and such abominable words as no Christian ear can endure to hear.

HENRY VI, PART 2
4. 7. 36–39

You are a rare parrot-teacher.

MUCH ADO ABOUT NOTHING
1. 1. 128

Thy words are blunt, and so art thou.

HENRY VI, PART 2
4. 1. 67

Come, you are a tedious fool. To the purpose.

MEASURE FOR MEASURE
2. 1. 115

(You) speak an infinite deal of nothing.

THE MERCHANT OF VENICE
1. 1. 113

Duller than a great thaw.

MUCH ADO ABOUT NOTHING
2. 1. 228

She speaks, yet she says nothing.

ROMEO AND JULIET
2. 2. 12

Thou dost talk nothing to me.

THE TEMPEST
2. 1. 16

I profit not by thy talk.

TROILUS AND CRESSIDA
5. 1. 13

BECAUSE BOREDOM ALONE cannot guarantee docility in students, and indeed can build up explosive pressures in the young, teachers must always combine boredom with tyranny.

The most effective methods of tyranny involve handing people a goal and convincing them to control themselves. Hence the idea that education, social life, and future income are all bound up together. If the teacher says you've failed at something you couldn't care less about, you start to worry you have lost out on a good life. This is meant to make students work hard at filling their heads with education and sociable behavior. But this threat of being cast forever into "the staggers and the careless lapse/Of youth and ignorance" (*All's Well That Ends Well*) is mild propaganda next to the administration's actual power to expel. The full force of the state awaits any acts of truly breathtaking creativity.

Creativity that cannot be penalized comes from a boisterous imagination that educators have inadvertently embraced and even championed—the democratic mind of Shakespeare. The authorities may not realize what they have done by giving their blessings to the Bard. His insults fly in the face of the strict and stodgy and release those who quote him from the iron fist.

How the fat rogue roared.

HENRY IV, PART 1
2. 2. 106

*She will die ere she will bate one breath
of her accustomed crossness.*

MUCH ADO ABOUT NOTHING
2. 3. 170–73

*You cram these words into mine ears
against the stomach of my sense.*

THE TEMPEST
2. 1. 102–3

What, no attendance? No regard? No duty?

THE TAMING OF THE SHREW
4. 1. 113

What! I say, my foot a tutor?

THE TEMPEST
1. 2. 471–72

*(My) care should be
To comb your noddle with a three-legg'd stool.*

THE TAMING OF THE SHREW

1. 1. 63–64

DAYS OF STARING into the glazed eyes of eager (to be elsewhere) students inspire all sorts of ideas. If even the mildest of professors' daydreams came to the attention of the law or of certain reporters for the tabloid press, all the world would live scandalized by the total weirdness of teachers. Prison populations would certainly have greater access to the time of previously busy tutors.

Intimations of what goes on in a teacher's mind are often found in external evidence. That pair of lucky trousers worn every day, that particularly greasy coiffure, the squeaky left shoe, the herbivorous halitosis (spinach in the teeth, and the like), the fanfare of tics and lisps. These are a sample of the sorts of indicators of oddity that students cannot ignore.

Shakespeare, of course, had no idea that the plays he was writing would become masterpieces fussed over by millions of educators. If he had known his personal stage would be global, he would have done what we have: ranged a broadside of insults to fire

off at the human race's collective strangeness, the entirety of which resides in micro-
cosm somewhere in the unassuming mind of
every teacher.

The really odd and sad thing about teachers, from a student's viewpoint, is that they
haven't a clue how bizarre they are. Some of
the more self-aware have taken refuge in the
comforting thought that strangeness is
highly valued by the young. But they are
dreaming. There is weird, and then there is
weird. The insults in this collection apply to
all teachers who perfect their own distinctive
styles of oddity.

Were't not for laughing I should pity him.

HENRY IV, PART 1
2. 2. 105

*I find the ass in compound with the major
part of your syllables.*

CORIOLANUS
2. 1. 57–58

This is the very coinage of your brain.

HAMLET
3. 4. 139

*He is as valiant as the lion, churlish as the
bear, slow as the elephant: a man into whom
nature has so crowded humours that his
valour is crushed into folly, his folly sauced
with discretion. There is no man hath a
virtue that he hath not a glimpse of, nor any
man an attaint but he carries some stain of
it. He is melancholy without cause and merry
against the hair; he hath the joints of
everything, but everything so out of joint that
he is a gouty Briareus, many hands and no
use, or purblind Argus, all eyes and no sight.*

TROILUS AND CRESSIDA
1. 2. 20–31

If his name be George, I'll call him Peter.

KING JOHN
1. 1. 186

*Here's a large mouth indeed,
That spits forth death and mountains,
rocks and seas,
Talks as familiarly of roaring lions
As maids of thirteen do of puppy-dogs!*

KING JOHN
2. 1. 457–60

(You are) the scarecrow that affrights
our children so.

HENRY VI, PART 1
1. 4. 42

With many holiday and lady terms
He question'd me.

HENRY IV, PART 1
1. 3. 45–46

I never knew man hold vile stuff so dear.

LOVE'S LABOUR'S LOST
4. 3. 273

His words are a very fantastical banquet,
just so many strange dishes.

MUCH ADO ABOUT NOTHING
2. 3. 20–21

To be so odd and from all fashions
cannot be commendable.

MUCH ADO ABOUT NOTHING
3. 1. 72–73

Goodly Lord, what a wit-snapper are you!

THE MERCHANT OF VENICE
3. 5. 45

(You are) a fellow o' th' strangest mind i' th'
world.

TWELFTH NIGHT
1. 3. 110–11

There's a stewed phrase indeed!

TROILUS AND CRESSIDA
3. 1. 40–41

OBSTRUCTIONIST ADMINISTRATORS

AN ADMINISTRATOR IS the ideal former student. This is literally true, because education officials everywhere design systems to turn out people just like themselves. The small conference room is the faint heart; the classroom the weak pulse. With every committee meeting, more responsibility is avoided and a bit more risk is eliminated from the life of the student. Danger lies in any new idea, for the obvious reason that the effects of innovation are unproven. What stand proven are current methods, regardless of their results, because the whole structure of procedure and authority exists, and it would not exist if current methods were ineffective. If changes would ever be required, unlikely as that is, the current system must be given enough chance to work, particularly if it has never worked yet.

It is merely coincidental that present organizational structures also happen to be the basis of power that the administrators hold. Any innovation whatever would put some ambitious, young, and hence unproven upstart in a position to upset the balance.

Administrators, as well-behaved products of their own systems, cannot imagine that education might succeed with conflict and risk. When they prescribe Shakespeare studies, they are beguiled by his reputation for having been dead for nearly 400 years. This uncontroversial move, however, inadvertently arms living people to blandish insults, which only demonstrates how untrustworthy living people are.

(It) exceeds in goodness the hugeness
of your unworthy thinking.

CYMBELINE
1. 5. 149–50

You may as well go about to turn
the sun to ice with fanning in his face
with a peacock's feather.

HENRY V
4. 1. 205–7

I am whipp'd and scourg'd with rods,
ttled, and stung with pismires, when I hear
Of this vile politician.

HENRY IV, PART 1
1. 3. 237–39

I can hardly forbear hurling things at him.

TWELFTH NIGHT
3. 2. 78–79

I have borne, and borne, and borne, and
have been fubbed off, and fubbed off, and
fubbed off, from this day to that day, that it is
a shame to be thought on.

HENRY IV, PART 2
2. 1. 32–35

Y'are lazy knaves, and here ye lie baiting of
bombards when ye should do service.

HENRY VIII
5. 3. 79–81

Thou fortune's champion, that dost never fight
But when her humorous ladyship is by
To teach thee safety!

KING JOHN
3. 1. 44–46

(You) whoreson beetle-headed,
flap-ear'd knave!

THE TAMING OF THE SHREW
4. 1. 144

*He is a proper man's picture, but alas! who
can converse with a dumb-show?*

THE MERCHANT OF VENICE
1. 2. 69–70

(You) slave, who never yields us kind answer!

THE TEMPEST
1. 2. 310–11

*I will do nothing at thy bidding.
Make thy requests to thy friend.*

TIMON OF ATHENS
1. 1. 267–68

POMPOUS ADMINISTRATORS

ADMINISTRATORS ARE NOT actually
pompous or stupid. This is mere affectation,
it is deliberately and almost universally nur-
tured as a means of diverting attention from
their true intentions in order to get their way
without opposition. In other words, it is
equivalent to boredom as used by teachers.

Administrators fancy themselves as minor
Machiavellians. Their trade is political
power, the open face of which looks very
much indeed like pompous stupidity. But

POMPOUS ADMINISTRATORS **35**

there are actually about as many stupid politicians as there are wise ones, which is very few. Unfortunately, politics requires suspicion, hence distrust, and hence preemptive oppression. The driving force in the administrator's being, then, is self-preservation.

Self-defense in itself is no vice, of course, but a whole bureaucracy made of it can be imposing. Shakespeare offers verbal weapons to anyone courageous enough to cut through this administrative creativity—or even to mutter boldly about administrators behind their backs.

What a wretched and peevish fellow is he,
to mope with his fat-brained followers
so far out of his knowledge!

HENRY V
3 . 7 . 133–35

Here is a silly-stately style indeed!

HENRY VI, PART 1
4 . 7 . 72

Mend my company, take away thyself.

TIMON OF ATHENS
4 . 3 . 285

(Be) mocked for valiant ignorance,
and perish constant fools.

CORIOLANUS
4. 6. 105–6

(You) fortify in paper and in figures,
Using the names of men instead of men.

HENRY IV, PART 2
1. 3. 56–57

They flock together in consent,
like so many wild geese.

HENRY IV, PART 2
5. 1. 67–68

You are the fount that makes
small brooks to flow.

HENRY VI, PART 3
4. 8. 54

He is every man in no man.

THE MERCHANT OF VENICE
1. 2. 57

He takes false shadows for true substances.

TITUS ANDRONICUS
3. 2. 80

There are a sort of men whose visages
Do cream and mantle like a standing pond.

THE MERCHANT OF VENICE
1. 1. 88–89

Manhood is melted into curtsies, valour into
compliment, and men are only turned into
tongues, and trim ones too.

MUCH ADO ABOUT NOTHING
4. 1. 318–20

Thou wilt fall backward when
thou hast more wit.

ROMEO AND JULIET
1. 3. 42

(He), having his ear full of his airy fame,
Grows dainty of his worth.

TROILUS AND CRESSIDA
1. 3. 144–45

I had rather be a tick in a sheep
than such a valiant ignorance.

TROILUS AND CRESSIDA
3. 3. 309–10

INCOMPETENT ADMINISTRATORS

POINTING OUT someone's inability to do something not worth doing is, by accident of English grammar, a compliment. Double negative, and all that. And if the specious task has an important enough aura about it, exposing someone's incompetence might even be a high compliment. This is the best explanation why certain individuals devote themselves to academic administration. They regard their work as a high calling, and the river of criticism that flows mightily over them is the perpetual baptism of thankless-ness reserved for the saints.

The one small problem, easily overlooked early in a career, is that grammar and life are not the same thing. This mistake of assuming that language and life are related to one another is particularly prevalent among former English teachers, who have advanced beyond fiction to construct a modest incompetence in administation.

In fact although not in word, the double negative means twice as bad. And since there are more than twice as many administrators in education as there should be, the profession is irretrievably flawed.

Thou didst not, savage,
Know thine own meaning,
but wouldst gabble like
A thing most brutish.

THE TEMPEST
1. 2. 357–59

Your means are very slender,
and your waste is great.

HENRY IV, PART 2
1. 2. 139–40

He hath a killing tongue and a quiet sword;
by the means whereof he breaks words,
and keeps whole weapons.

HENRY V
3. 2. 35–37

(They are) noisome weeds which
without profit suck
The soil's fertility from wholesome flowers.

RICHARD II
3. 4. 38–39

Thou art no Atlas for so great a weight.

HENRY VI, PART 3

5. 1. 36

Thou hast most traitorously corrupted
the youth of the realm in erecting
a grammar-school.

HENRY VI, PART 2
4. 7. 30–32

I am sorry for thy much misgovernment.

MUCH ADO ABOUT NOTHING
4. 1. 99

It appears by his small light of discretion
that he is in the wane.

A MIDSUMMER NIGHT'S DREAM
5. 1. 243–44

Thou whoreson zed! thou unnecessary letter!

KING LEAR
2. 2. 64

There's small choice in rotten apples.

THE TAMING OF THE SHREW
1. 1. 134–35

If (the others) be brain'd like (you),
the state totters.

THE TEMPEST
3. 2. 6

STUDENTS

(They are) the children of

an idle brain,

Begot of nothing but

vain fantasy,

Which is as thin of

substance as the air

And more inconstant than

the wind.

ROMEO AND JULIET
1. 4. 97–100

LIKE ALMOST EVERYTHING ELSE, language itself collapses into groveling irony at the feet of students. The very word *student* shares roots with "study," which proves all is not as it seems. Young scholars—meaning "school attendees" or at least "on-the-rolls," or these days "able to direct strangers to within a half-mile of a local institution of any sort"—would be better designated by their clothes, music, body decoration, slang, and attitude than by their ability or willingness to study. "Attitudents," maybe. The only positive link they have to houses of learning is that governments and future employers (or fire-ers) collude in keeping them in one place for most of the day, where they are off the street and easier to control with professional handlers.

Although ignorance is a gift of nature (see the introduction for a lengthier description), real stupidity requires years of genuine commitment. Students fall somewhere in between. They are characterized by unbounded energy, short attention spans, and half-innocent optimism trying to appear as pessimism, all compressed into a mass of contradictory forces, unaccustomed body parts, and inner conflicts. School is a zoo-logical garden of the hormones: here a little *test-*, there a little *est-*, in not quite natural habitat. Coincidentally, this description of students is an almost perfect description of Shakespeare's plays. Much Shakespearean language lends itself to describe students as lazy, distracted, mischievous, and adept at making excuses—especially on report cards.

Lazy

LAZINESS IS A CHIMERA (a mythic beast, no more). Students may well have goats' bodies, serpents' tails and heads out of a Disney cartoon, but they never lack ded-ication, energy, or determination to achieve what is truly important. Only elders, beyond twenty-five years old, could fail to compre-hend their commitment.

More often than not, students are accused of indolence only because they stand firm against losing themselves in someone else's plans. Insults that confront the obvious exploit this misunderstanding of subtle virtue.

O monstrous beast, how like a swine he lies!

THE TAMING OF THE SHREW IND.

1. 32

You had measur'd how long a fool you
were upon the ground.

CYMBELINE
1. 3. 22–23

Every day that comes comes to decay
a day's work in him.

CYMBELINE
1. 6. 56–57

(You) apes of idleness!

HENRY IV, PART 2
4. 5. 122

Repair thy wit good youth, or it will fall
To cureless ruin.

THE MERCHANT OF VENICE
4. 1. 141–42

Thy brains
(Are) useless, boil'd within thy skull!

THE TEMPEST
5. 1. 59–60

There will little learning die then that day
thou art hang'd.

TIMON OF ATHENS
2. 2. 85–86

How have you come so early by this lethargy!

TWELFTH NIGHT
1. 5. 124–25

O illiterate loiterer!

THE TWO GENTLEMEN OF VERONA
3. 1. 290

DISTRACTED

SEX IS NOT ALWAYS the topic being addressed in school. It is this flaw in the curriculum that causes students to appear distracted when they are not.

A teacher need only make a passing reference to any figure of speech that can be remotely conjoined with any carnal innuendo to discover where the hearts, minds, hands, and assorted other parts of students are occupied. There is never a lack of imagination in any teaching situation. There is only a prudish refusal to acknowledge where that imagination lies.

The student's apparent lack of attention arouses the ill temper of older and apparently wiser persons who have lost their own youthful appetites. They now crave other forms of attention (or non-distraction) them-

selves. These pathetic, decrepit, and poten-
tially degenerate individuals can take fiery
words of Shakespeare to keep them warm.

*Bless me, what a fry of fornication is at the
door!*

HENRY VIII
5. 3. 34–35

Be not lost so poorly in your thoughts.

MACBETH
2. 2. 70–71

*(You are) an index and prologue to the
history of lust and foul thoughts.*

OTHELLO
2. 1. 254–55

*Would the fountain of your mind were clear
again, that I might water an ass at it.*

TROILUS AND CRESSIDA
3. 3. 308–9

MISCHIEVOUS

MOST TROUBLE, for which students are
justly famous, is the product of high energy
and erratic concentration. The suspected

Thy head stands so tickle on thy shoulders,
that a milk-maid, if she be in love,
may sigh it off.

MEASURE FOR MEASURE
1. 2. 161–63

perpetrators always seem doltish when questioned by authorities, who always point out at length in clever hindsightful rhetoric that the inevitable is preventable. It rarely is. Trouble will pursue humankind eternally, and so for efficiency's sake, there is a need to prepare long-winded lectures in advance for those occasions when young people do rash and mindless things.

Not all trouble is inadvertent, however. A streak of adult behavior begins to appear at an early age. Although not yet up to practicing the myriad forms of full-fledged venality, students find that simple mischief holds a compelling attractiveness. This youthful delight in trouble-making is almost never seen for what it is—experimentation with creativity that will mature into things like cures for cancer and formulas for world peace. Instead, delight is rudely and short-sightedly suppressed in the interest of eradicating such methods of expression as graffiti, armed robbery, disrespectful gestures, drug dealing, extortion, burglary, car theft, shoplifting, and mayhem.

Such is thy audacious wickedness,
Thy lewd, pestiferous, and dissentious pranks,
As very infants prattle of thy pride!

HENRY VI, PART 1
3. 1. 14–16

How many fruitless pranks
This ruffian hath botch'd up.

TWELFTH NIGHT
4. 1. 54–55

(You are) scambling, outfacing, fashion-
monging boys,
That lie, and cog, and flout, deprave,
and slander,
Go anticly, and show outward hideousness,
And speak off half a dozen dang'rous words,
How (you) might hurt (your) enenmies, if
(you) durst,
And this is all.

MUCH ADO ABOUT NOTHING
5. 1. 94–99

Here's a young and sweating devil here,
That commonly rebels.

OTHELLO
3. 4. 38–39

(You're) such a want-wit!

THE MERCHANT OF VENICE
1. 1. 6

Such short-liv'd wits do wither as they grow.

LOVE'S LABOUR'S LOST
2. 1. 54

Since she could speak,
She hath not given so many
good words breath.

TROILUS AND CRESSIDA
4. 1. 73–74

These gentlemen are of such sensible
and nimble lungs that they always
use to laugh at nothing.

THE TEMPEST
2. 1. 168–70

Boys, with women's voices, strive to speak big.

RICHARD II
3. 2. 113–14

You heedless joltheads and
unmanner'd slaves!

THE TAMING OF THE SHREW
4. 1. 153

Hell is empty,
And all the devils are here.

THE TEMPEST
1. 2. 214–15

Is there no manners left among maids?

THE WINTER'S TALE
4. 4. 244

If our wits run the wild-goose chase
I am done. For thou hast more of the wild-
goose in one of thy wits than I am sure
I have in my whole five.

ROMEO AND JULIET
2. 4. 72–74

I would there were no age between ten and
three-and-twenty, or that youth would sleep
out the rest; for there is nothing in the
between but getting wenches with child,
wronging the ancientry, stealing, fighting.

THE WINTER'S TALE
3. 3. 59–63

EXCUSES

THERE ARE TWO APPROACHES students take in relation to teachers. Teachers establish standards and guide students to achieve them; students either do the work or make excuses.

We can ignore for the moment the few students who do the work and the even fewer who do it on time, not to say do it well. The great majority learn in school and university to make excuses. This serves them well in later life, which shows us that not all the tax money devoted to education is spent ineffectively after all. Like sex, excuse-making (listed in course books as "alibi engineering") is a major aspect of the educational enterprise that has yet to be formally recognized. A phased, staged, and modular way forward in this field is to borrow insights from Shakespeare, who is already on the curriculum.

(You have) a truant disposition.

HAMLET
1. 2. 169

That's somewhat madly spoken.

MEASURE FOR MEASURE
5. 1. 92

You do advance your cunning
more and more.

A MIDSUMMER NIGHT'S DREAM
3. 2. 128

If you be mad, be gone:
if you have reason, be brief.

TWELFTH NIGHT
1. 5. 200–1

You never spoke what did become
you less than this.

THE WINTER'S TALE
1. 2. 282–83

You tread upon my patience.

HENRY IV, PART 1
1. 3. 4.

REPORT CARDS

THE TIME, IF NOT THE EFFORT, that a student spends draining the country's education budget must be translated into official reports. These will be largely ignored or, if attended to, misinterpreted. Their great contribution is symbolically reducing otherwise unmanageable individuals to ciphers, while simultaneously reducing the person charged with writing them to a wreck of depleted imagination. The ordeal of report writing keeps teachers exhausted and subservient to the relentless devices of administrators.

The teacher's drudgery is driven by fear that parents of different students will compare reports and find identical comments. Originality is absolutely required, even when creativity is on the wane. Content matters little, but each person's individuality must be affirmed. The top and bottom of the class are child's play—the same message with different adjectives. The students in the middle pose the challenge. But now the jaded teacher need only copy any of the following comments verbatim. With no effort at all, everyone's unique qualities will come to life for even the keenest administrator or parent.

(You are) a slight unmeritable man,
meet to be sent on errands.

JULIUS CAESAR
4. 1. 12–13

(You are) one that converses more
with the buttock of the night than with
the forehead of the morning.

CORIOLANUS
2. 1. 50–52

She was a vixen when she went to school,
And though she be but little, she is fierce.

A MIDSUMMER NIGHT'S DREAM
3. 2. 324–25

He is a thing too bad for bad report.

CYMBELINE
1. 1. 16—17

What a lack-brain is this!

HENRY IV, PART 1
2. 3. 16

*(He) wears his wit in his belly
and his guts in his head.*

TROILUS AND CRESSIDA
2. 1. 75—76

*His addiction was to courses vain;
His companies unletter'd, rude, and shallow;
His hours fill'd up with riots, banquets, sports;
And never noted in him any study,
Any retirement, any sequestration
From open haunts and popularity.*

HENRY V
1. 1. 54—59

*(You have an) undressed, unpolished,
uneducated, unpruned, untrained, or rather
unlettered, or ratherest, unconfirmed fashion.*

LOVE'S LABOUR'S LOST
4. 2. 16—19

He's more, had I more name for badness.

MEASURE FOR MEASURE
5. 1. 61–62

All in vain comes counsel to his ear.

RICHARD II
2. 1. 4

Thou art not altogether a fool.

TIMON OF ATHENS
2. 2. 119

The cur is excellent at faults.

TWELFTH NIGHT
2. 5. 128–29

There's a stewed phrase indeed!
There's a stewed phrase indeed!

TROILUS AND CRESSIDA
3. 1. 40–41

(You are) a fellow o' th' strangest mind
i' th' world.

TWELFTH NIGHT
1. 3. 110–11

PARENTS

Thou mad misleader of thy

brain-sick son!

HENRY VI, PART 2
5. 1. 163

PARENTS BEHAVE EXACTLY like teachers and administrators except that they are outside the education system and are unpaid (which some consider to be proper remuneration for teachers and administrators). As much as volunteer help is appreciated in any large and financially stretched organization, its quality can be inconsistent. In some circumstances, even detrimental. Well-intentioned parents who take the time to expound the rudiments of rocket science, brain surgery, or basket weaving to their offspring inevitably leave out the crucial parts. With no mention of modules, key stages, learning objectives, or facilitator milestones, only confusion can result. And confusion is the proper function of paid staff.

The most important parental contributions to the business of education are indifference, prejudice, hostility, and providing bad examples. That way students have a chance to learn by their own mistakes, which is what they would have liked all along.

INDIFFERENCE IS THE ADULT version of distraction. With uncontrollable sex drives long ago gone stampeding over the horizon, little excitement remains to cloud mature judgment. Parents are thus well positioned to enrich the vocational education of their children. Adults are experts in the headlong chase after whatever happens to be urgent at the moment. The special skills of disillusionment with life's larger opportunities, combined with a wisdom born of conversion to the self-accepting satisfactions of membership in the television audience, make parents ideal advocates of neglect.

The apathetic attitude appears in all periods of human history. Shakespeare in his day had words for its exemplars, and these comments are still useful today, for jaded parents of smarmy children.

(You) repent not in ashes and sackcloth,
but in new silk and old sack.

HENRY IV, PART 2
1. 2. 196–98

(You are) a vane blown with all winds.

MUCH ADO ABOUT NOTHING

3. 1. 66

Such a dish of skim milk!

HENRY IV, PART 1
2. 3. 33

*Such toasts-and-butter, with hearts in their
bellies no bigger than pins' heads.*

HENRY IV, PART 1
4. 2. 20–22

*You are all recreants and dastards, and
delight to live in slavery.*

HENRY VI, PART 2
4. 8. 28–29

Hang! Beg! Starve! Die in the streets!

ROMEO AND JULIET
3. 5. 192

I have said too much unto a heart of stone.

TWELFTH NIGHT
3. 4. 203

*(Thou art not) altogether a wise man.
As much foolery as I have,
so much wit thou lacks't.*

TIMON OF ATHENS
2. 2. 120–21

One of thy kin has a most weak pia mater.

TWELFTH NIGHT
1. 5. 115–16

This house is as dark as ignorance,
though ignorance were as dark as hell.

TWELFTH NIGHT
4. 2. 46–47

PREJUDICED AND BLAMING

PARENT-TEACHER conferences show the results earlier teachers were able to achieve, for the parent too had education done to him or her. Here is an individual officially integrated into society and the national culture. In all likelihood, the parent is what the student will turn out to be. But the teacher has little time to stare the future in the face, for the future is sitting there complaining.

By refusing to participate in the student's education, parents deftly avoid even a hint of blame for any of its imperfections. With perfectly clear consciences, they unleash their considered opinions against the work of the teacher. "Not my child!" is the sullen refrain. Always there is much to criticize, but there are limits of good taste. Even for parents it is bad form to sink to the level of the obvious by lumping teachers with administration and tarring the lot. This cheap move is not uncommon, no matter how unconvincing.

Parental hostility has nothing to do with the education of the present generation of students. Instead, it is an eruption of memory. The cycle is as follows: go to school, hate the teacher, wait, take it out on your kid's teacher. Since precision was always demanded in school, the retribution is sweeter if accompanied by confusion. Hence the value of Shakespeare. Memorizing even a one- or two-line insult just before meeting the teacher, and misquoting it slightly to lend it the authenticity of a distant memory, can give the impression of learning in the midst of a highly prejudiced attack against it. It is ironic that exactly the same insults work equally well in the mouths of teachers against parents as vice versa.

*(These) groundlings for the most part
are capable of nothing but inexplicable
dumb-shows and noise.*

HAMLET

3. 2. 11–12

They are arrant knaves, and will backbite.

HENRY IV, PART 2

5. 1. 30

Here he comes, swelling like a turkey-cock.

HENRY V

5. 1. 15–16

Shall I be flouted thus by dunghill grooms?

HENRY VI, PART 1

1. 3. 14

(You) riddling merchant!

HENRY VI, PART 1

2. 3. 56

*Can (I) endure to hear this arrogance?
And from this fellow?*

HENRY VIII

3. 2. 278–79

The tartness of his face sours ripe grapes.

CORIOLANUS
5. 4. 17–18

Thou hast no speculation in those eyes,
Which thou dost glare with.

MACBETH
3. 4. 94–95

A gentle riddance, draw the curtains, go.

THE MERCHANT OF VENICE
2. 7. 78

What impossible matter
will he make easy next?

THE TEMPEST
2. 1. 85

(This) is as fat and fulsome to mine ear
As howling after music.

TWELFTH NIGHT
5. 1. 107–8

If you spend word for word with me,
I shall make your wit bankrupt.

THE TWO GENTLEMEN OF VERONA
2. 4. 37–38

Setting a Poor Example

THE ADVENT OF EDUCATIONAL television has placed parents in a dilemma. Should the usual sex and violence be shunned for a small-screen spin around the chemistry laboratory? How can blowing things up improve the quality of life at the end of the millennium? The same authorities that encroach upon the young all day have crept smiling into the house at night.

Parents who presume to extend learning into the home might be risking the mental health of their children. Those are no ordinary teachers on the tube; they might even be actors. And any normal adult who sits in front of educational television is certainly an actor, if not an extra, and in any case will not be normal long.

Bad examples should be gross, palpable, and fragrant. Otherwise, what is the point?

*Let the doors be shut upon him, that he may
play the fool nowhere but in's own house.*

HAMLET

3. 1. 133–34

Well, the truth is you live in great infamy.

HENRY IV, PART 2

1. 2. 135–36

*It is certain that either wise bearing or
ignorant carriage is caught, as men take
diseases, one of another.*

HENRY IV, PART 2

5. 1. 72–74

He be as good a gentleman as the devil is.

HENRY V

4. 7. 141–42

*(They are) hard-handed men which never
labor'd in their minds till now.*

A MIDSUMMER NIGHT'S DREAM

5. 1. 72–73

*Having flown over many knavish professions,
he settled only in rogue.*

THE WINTER'S TALE

4. 3. 95–96

Foolery, sir, does walk about the orb like the sun, it shines everywhere.

TWELFTH NIGHT
3. 1. 39–40

Men from children nothing differ.

MUCH ADO ABOUT NOTHING
5. 1. 33

(He's) a gentleman that loves to hear himself talk, and will speak more in a minute than he will stand to in a month.

ROMEO AND JULIET
2. 4. 144–46

CONCLUSION

We have a friend who, whether from a twisted sense of justice or not we do not know, devoted several hours each week attempting to inflict learning upon the young villains (as Britain's junior convicts are known) in one of Her Majesty's prisons. Things were going badly with the syllabus, until she stood bolt upright and declared, "If you're going to curse, you're going to do it properly!"

She brought our collection of *Shakespeare's Insults* to the next session. Rarely in prison history has a work with literary pretensions been borrowed so frequently or dog-eared so quickly. One of the young offenders was able to make a name for himself by starting a riot in which the *Evening News* caught him calling the prison governor a "king of codpieces." In the confusion, all members of the seminar effected a successful escape.

We suspect they have passed themselves off as educated personages (the ultimate disguise), for they have never been recaptured. Shakespeare has since been banned from

H.M. Prison Service and legislated instead into every school in the hope that more young people will pass with similar alacrity out the doors of another costly and scandalously governed institution.